RESPONSIVE
DESIGN

All CSS Features for Adaptive Layou

Abdelfatt Ragab

Responsive Design

All CSS Features for Adaptive Layouts

Abdelfattah Ragab

Introduction

Welcome to the book "Responsive Design: All CSS functions for adaptive layouts". In this book, I'll explain all the CSS functions you need to know to create adaptive layouts.

Adaptive layouts are layouts that change depending on the screen width or device orientation. We usually refer to them as responsive design.

By the end of this book, you'll know which features to use and be able to handle all kinds of scenarios.

Let's go

Run on all devices

It would be great if you could develop your application just once and then run it on all devices.
You can achieve this by applying some CSS rules. In this book, I'll introduce you to all the CSS rules you can use to ensure that your app works smoothly on all devices and adapts to any screen size. Here is an example page:

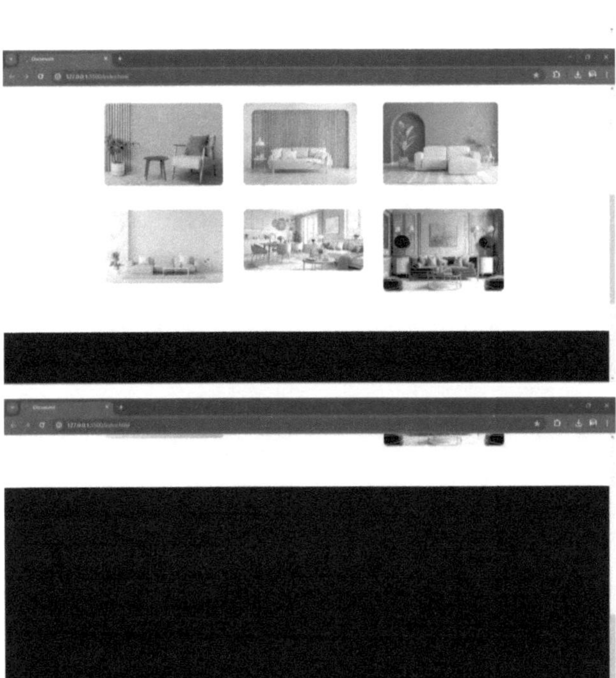

The page has the following parts

```
<!-- header -->
<!-- featured -->
```

```html
<!-- items -->
<!-- footer -->
```

The HTML document

Here is the original HTML document with the title, the logo and the link to the style.css file.

HTML
```html
<!DOCTYPE html>
<html lang="en">
  <head>
    <meta charset="UTF-8" />
    <meta name="viewport"
content="width=device-width, initial-scale=1.0"
/>
    <title>Shrova Mall</title>
    <link rel="stylesheet" href="style.css" />
    <link rel="shortcut icon"
href="assets/images/logo.png" type="image/png"
/>
  </head>
  <body></body>
</html>
```

CSS
```css
html,
body {
  padding: 0;
  margin: 0;
}
```

In the browser it looks like this, a blank page with title and favicon

The header

In the body element, we add our first element, the header

HTML

```html
    <div class="header">
      <div class="brand">
        <img class="logo"
src="assets/images/logo.png" alt="" />
        <div class="brand-name">Shrova
Mall</div>
      </div>
    </div>
```

CSS

```css
.header {
  width: 100%;
  height: 80px;
  display: flex;
  justify-content: flex-start;
```

```css
    align-items: center;
    font-family: Arial, Helvetica, sans-serif;
    padding: 0 30px;
    box-sizing: border-box;
    box-shadow: 0 0 2px 2px gray;
    margin-bottom: 2px;
    @media (min-width: 760px) {
      padding: 0 100px;
    }
}
.brand {
    display: flex;
    align-items: center;
    gap: 16px;
}
.brand-name {
    font-size: 2em;
    cursor: pointer;
}
.logo {
    width: 50px;
    cursor: pointer;
}
```

The header component has only one group of
components, the brand group, which consists of two
elements, the logo and the brand name.
For the header component, display has been set to flex
and justify-content to flex-start so that the brand group is
left-aligned.
There are two elements within the brand group, so the
brand group itself again has the display set to flex and
16px space between the logo and the brand name. The

align-items property ensures that all items are aligned vertically in the center.
There are so many details about the flexible layout that I have dedicated an entire book to this layout.

The featured Image

HTML

```html
<picture class="featured">
  <source
    class="featured-image"
    media="(min-width:760px)"
    srcset="assets/images/home-large.png"
  />
  <img class="featured-image"
src="assets/images/home-mobile.png" alt="" />
</picture>
```

CSS

```css
.featured-image {
  max-width: 100%;
}
```

S Shrova Mall
OUR WOODEN CONCEPTS:
Sustainable Furniture
Lorem ipsum dolor sit amet, consectetur adipiscing elit, sed do eiusmod tempor incididunt ut labore et dolore magna aliqua. Ut enim ad minim veniam quis.
DISCOVER MORE

Shrova Mall
S Shrova Mall
OUR WOODEN CONCEPTS:
Sustainable Furniture
Lorem ipsum dolor sit amet, consectetur adipiscing elit, sed do eiusmod tempor incididunt ut labore et dolore magna aliqua. Ut enim ad minim veniam quis.
DISCOVER MORE

This time we use the HTML picture element to use different images for different screen sizes.

The items

HTML

```html
<div class="items">
  <img class="item"
src="assets/images/image-001.avif" alt="" />
  <img class="item"
src="assets/images/image-002.avif" alt="" />
  <img class="item"
src="assets/images/image-003.avif" alt="" />
  <img class="item"
src="assets/images/image-004.avif" alt="" />
  <img class="item"
src="assets/images/image-005.avif" alt="" />
  <img class="item"
src="assets/images/image-006.avif" alt="" />
</div>
```

CSS

```css
.items {
  width: 100%;
  margin: auto;
  padding: 80px 40px;
  display: grid;
  grid-template-columns: repeat(2, 1fr);
  column-gap: 40px;
  row-gap: 80px;
  box-sizing: border-box;
  @media (min-width: 760px) {
    padding: 100px;
```

```css
    width: 80%;
    grid-template-columns: repeat(3, 1fr);
    row-gap: 60px;
  }
}
img.item {
  max-width: 100%;
  max-height: 200px;
  object-fit: contain;
  border-radius: 10px;
  cursor: pointer;
  @media (min-width: 760px) {
    max-width: 300px;
  }
}
img.item:hover {
  filter: brightness(1.1);
}
```

Furniture

Lorem ipsum dolor sit amet, consectetur adipiscing elit, sed do eiusmod tempor incididunt ut labore et dolore magna aliqua. Ut enim ad minim veniam quis.

DISCOVER MORE

There are 6 pieces of furniture that we will display on the screen. This time I will use the grid layout to distribute the images nicely on the screen.
I will use media queries to apply different columns of the grid template for different screen sizes. For mobile devices I will use a two-column template, while on large screens I will use 3 columns.

The footer

HTML

```
    <footer class="footer">
      <div class="copyright">©2024 by Shrova
Mall, all rights reserved.</div>
    </footer>
```

CSS

```
.footer {
  width: 100%;
  height: 600px;
  background-color: rgb(27, 27, 27);
  font-family: Arial, Helvetica, sans-serif;
  position: relative;
}
.copyright {
  color: rgb(226, 226, 226);
  position: absolute;
  text-align: center;
  bottom: 30px;
  width: 100%;
  cursor: default;
}
```

The height of the footer is 600px and the position is set to relative. The position of the subordinate copyright element is absolute and the lower value is set to 30px.

As you can see, we were able to create a nice responsive design with just a few lines of code for HTML and CSS.
You can work on it further, e.g. you can add another group for menu items in the header in addition to the brand group. In this case, set justify-content to space-between instead of flex-start to distribute the space between the two groups so that the brand group is on the left and the menu group is on the right.

Now you have an idea of how you can use HTML and CSS functions together to create a responsive design. On the next few pages, I will introduce you to all the functions you can use for a responsive design.

Here are the topics that I will explain to you on the following pages:
- Viewport Units (vw,vh,vmin,vmax)
- Relative Length Units (em, rem, and percent)
- Flexible Box Layout
- Grid Layout
- Media queries
- Multi-column layout (for newspapers and magazines)
- Responsive images (srcset and sizes attributes in HTML and CSS object-fit and object-position properties)

- Fluid typography (vw, vh, clamp())
- Media Query Features (min-width, max-width, orientation, resolution, aspect-ratio)
- Fluid Layouts

Viewport Units (vw,vh,vmin,vmax)

CSS viewport units are length units that refer to the size of the browser viewport. They allow you to create responsive designs that adapt to different screen sizes. There are four types of viewport units: vw, vh, vmin and vmax. Here you can find out what each unit means:

- **vw:** Represents 1% of the width of the viewport. For example, 50vw corresponds to 50% of the width of the viewport.
- **vh:** Stands for 1 % of the height of the viewport. For example, 50vh would correspond to 50% of the height of the viewport.
- **vmin:** Represents the smaller value between vw and vh. It is equal to the smaller of the two values. For example, if the width of the viewport is smaller than its height, 50vmin would be equal to 50% of the width of the viewport.
- **vmax:** Represents the larger value between vw and vh. It is equal to the larger of the two values. For example, if the width of the viewport is greater than its height, 50vmax would be equal to 50% of the width of the viewport.

These units are particularly useful for creating responsive designs that adapt to different screen sizes.

Viewport units can be used in various CSS properties, such as width, height, padding and margin. They allow you to dynamically adjust the size of elements to the size of the viewport. With the units vw and vh, for example, you can ensure that an element fills the entire size of the screen.

Viewport units are responsive, i.e. their value changes every time the browser is resized. This makes them incredibly useful for resizing elements in CSS and creating designs that adapt to different devices and screen sizes.

Relative Length Units (em, rem, and percent)

CSS offers several relative length units that you can use to specify sizes relative to other elements or properties. The three most commonly used relative length units are em, rem, and percent. We'll take a closer look at each of these units:

Em unit
The em unit is a relative length unit based on the font size of the next parent element. When you nest

elements, each level can have a different font size depending on the size of the parent element, resulting in different sizes. The em unit is often used to set font sizes, margins and padding. It is also useful for creating scalable and responsive designs.

Rem unit

The rem unit is a relative length unit that refers to the font size of the root element (html). Unlike the em unit, which refers to the nearest parent element, the rem unit remains consistent regardless of where it is used in the document. This makes it particularly useful for creating consistent and scalable designs across different elements and components.

Percent unit

The percent unit is a relative unit of length that represents a percentage of another value. In CSS, percentages are often used to specify widths, heights and other dimensions relative to the size of the parent element or viewport. For example, if you specify a width of 50% for an element, it will take up half the width of the parent element.

Comparison and use
- The em unit refers to the font size of the next parent element, while the rem unit refers to the font size of the root element.
- The em unit can lead to different sizes when nested, while the rem unit remains consistent throughout the document.

- Percentages refer to a different value, e.g. the size of the parent element or the dimensions of the viewport.

When choosing between the units em, rem and percent, you should note the following:
- Use the em unit if you want to scale the sizes relative to the font size of the next parent element.
- Use the rem unit if the sizes are to be scaled relative to the font size of the root element and consistency is to be maintained.
- Use the percentage unit if the sizes are to be scaled relative to another value, e.g. to the size of the parent element or to the dimensions of the viewport.

It is important to note that the choice of relative length unit depends on the particular application and design requirements. To achieve the desired results, it may be necessary to experiment and test.

Flexible Box Layout

CSS Flexible Box Layout, commonly referred to as Flexbox, is a layout model introduced in CSS3 that provides a flexible and efficient way to arrange and align elements within a container. It is designed to simplify the creation of complex and responsive layouts without relying on floats or positioning.

Flexbox allows you to distribute space among items in a container and control their alignment, order, and size. It is particularly useful for creating dynamic and adaptive layouts that can adjust to different screen sizes and orientations.

Example

We have 5 div elements with different sizes and colors as follows. By setting display flex in their wrapper, they are displayed as follows:

Before applying display flex to the wrapper, they looked like this

Now let's understand how flex layout works.

Flex layout has two main axes, the main axis and the cross axis

The main axis is defined by the flex-direction property, and the cross axis is perpendicular to it.

flex-direction can have four values: row, column, row-reverse and column-reverse.

if flex-direction is not specified, it is set to row by default

row

Default value. The flexible items are displayed horizontally, as a row

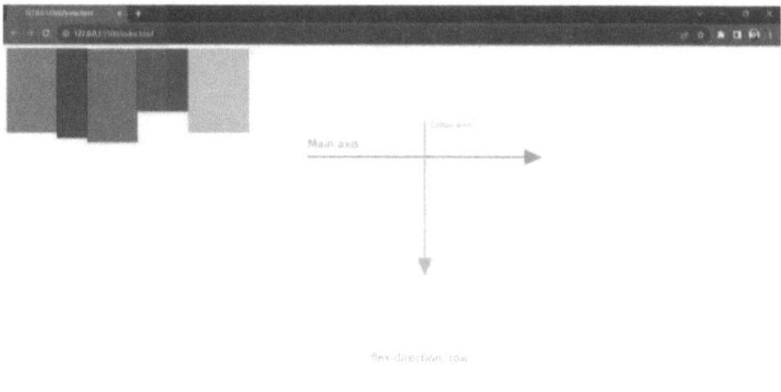

```css
.wrapper {
  display: flex;
  flex-direction: row;
}
```

row-reverse

Same as row, but in reverse order

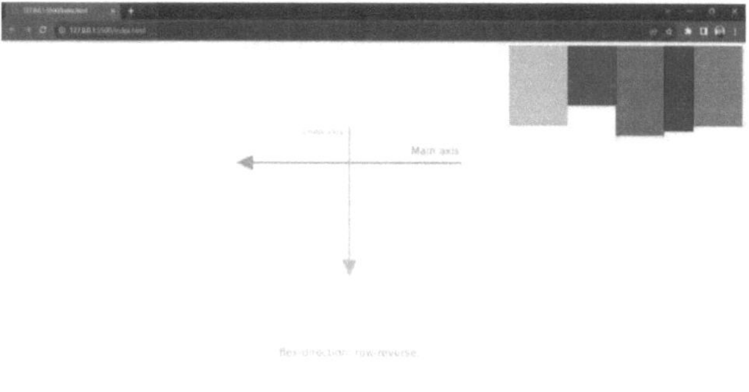

```css
.wrapper {
  display: flex;
```

```
flex-direction: row-reverse;
}
```

column

The flexible items are displayed vertically, as a column

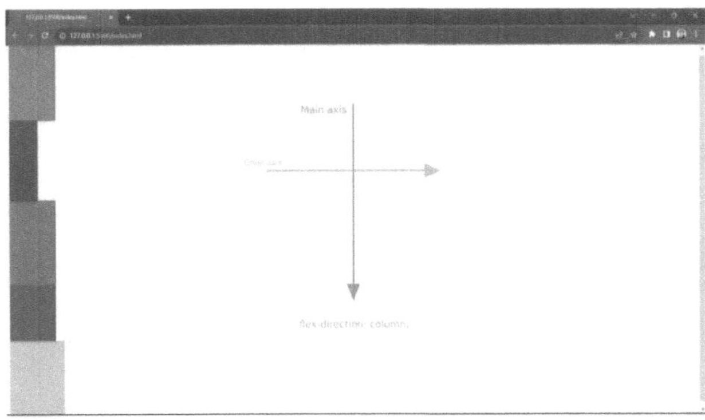


```
.wrapper {
  display: flex;
  flex-direction: column;
}
```

column-reverse

Same as column, but in reverse order

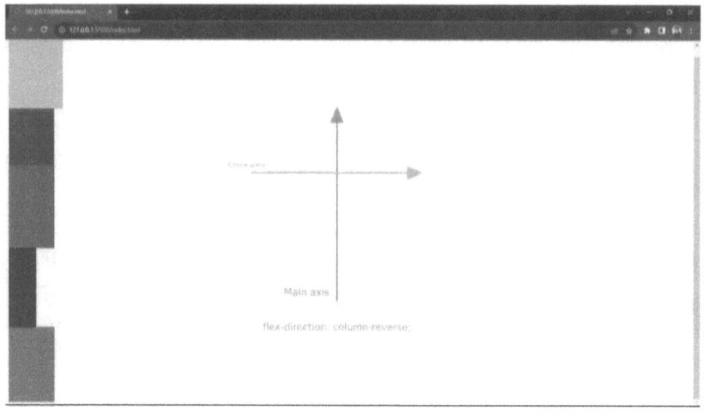


```css
.wrapper {
  display: flex;
  flex-direction: column-reverse;
}
```

Now let's look at how you can benefit from this, starting with two important flex layout properties justify-content and align-items.

justify-content

The CSS property justify-content determines how the browser distributes the space between and around content elements along the main axis of a flex container

flex-start

Default value. Items are positioned at the beginning of
the container

```
.wrapper {
  display: flex;
  flex-direction: row;
  justify-content: flex-start;
}
```

flex-end

Items are positioned at the end of the container

```css
.wrapper {
  display: flex;
  flex-direction: row;
  justify-content: flex-end;
}
```

center

Items are positioned in the center of the container

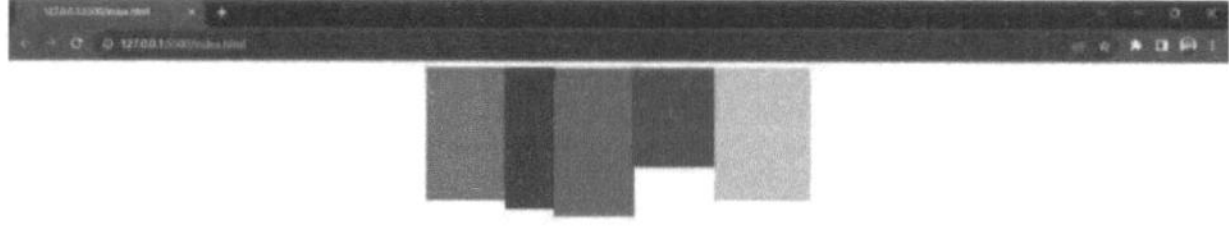

```css
.wrapper {
```

```css
    display: flex;

    flex-direction: row;

    justify-content: center;

  }
```

space-between

Items will have space between them

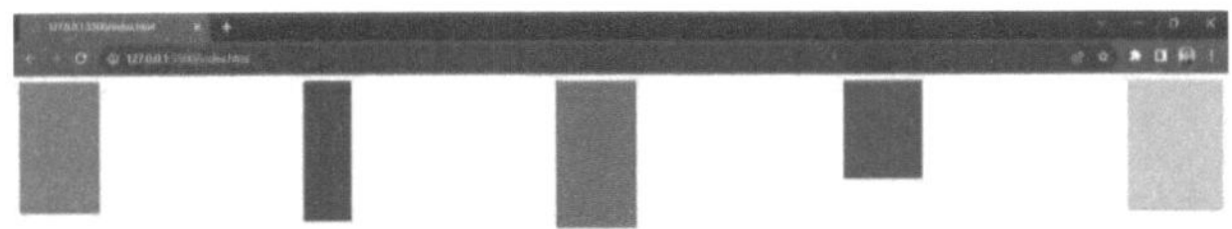

```css
  .wrapper {

    display: flex;

    flex-direction: row;

    justify-content: space-between;

  }

..
```

Please read my book **"CSS Flexbox Layout"** to learn all about the flexbox layout.

Grid Layout

CSS Grid Layout is a two-dimensional layout system that allows for the creation of grid-based layouts on webpages or applications. It provides a powerful and flexible way to arrange and position elements in both rows and columns. With CSS Grid Layout, developers have more control over the placement and alignment of elements, making it easier to create complex and responsive designs.

CSS Grid Layout was introduced in 2017 and has since gained popularity among web developers. It offers a range of properties and values that can be applied to grid containers and grid items to shape the layout.

We have an example with some div elements like this

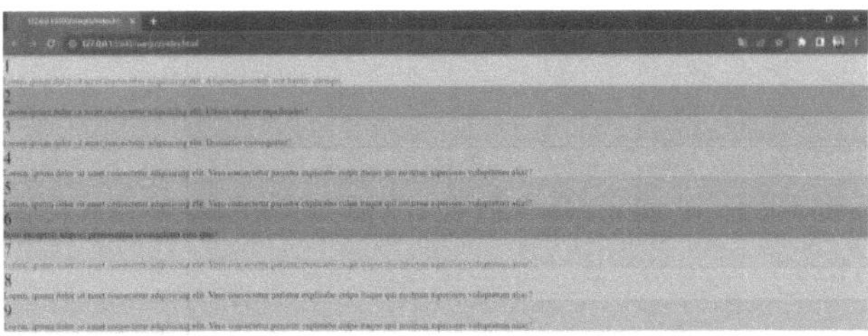

To make this a grid layout, I will set display: grid; to the container,

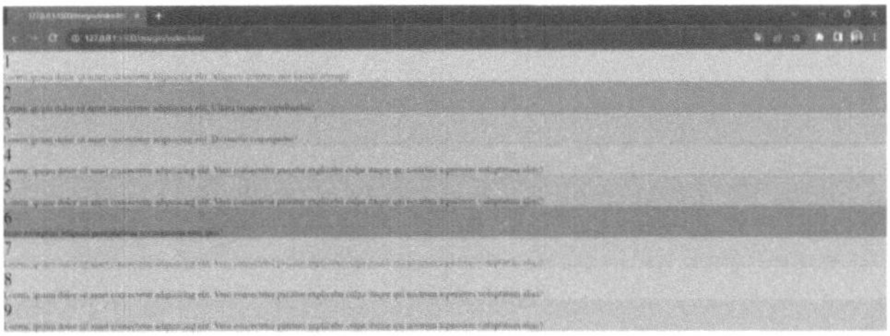

.wrapper {
    display: grid;
}

Now it is a grid layout, but it has no columns defined.

grid-template-columns

The grid-template-columns property defines the number (and width) of columns in a grid layout.

The values are a space-separated list in which each value specifies the size of the respective column.

none

Default value. Columns are created if needed

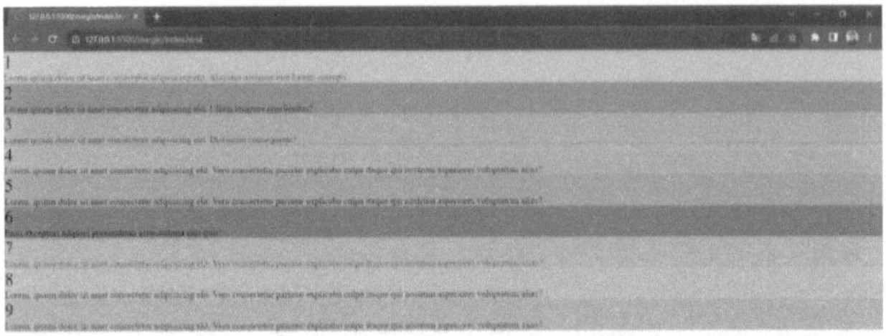

auto

The size of the columns depends on the size of the
container and the size of the content of the articles in
the column

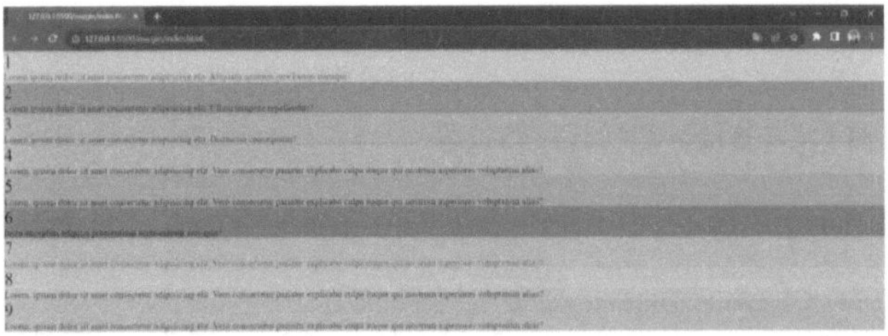

```css
.wrapper {
  display: grid;
  grid-template-columns: auto;
}
```

max-content

Sets the size of each column to depend on the largest item in the column

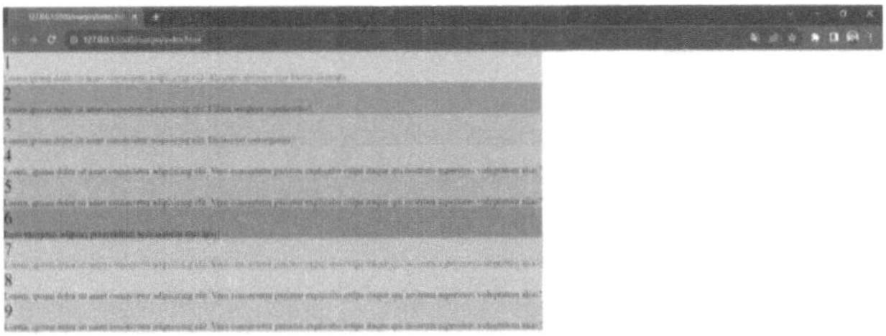

```
.wrapper {
  display: grid;
  grid-template-columns: max-content;
}
```

min-content

Sets the size of each column to depend on the smallest item in the column

```css
.wrapper {
  display: grid;
  grid-template-columns: min-content;
}
```

length

Sets the size of the columns, by using a legal length
value.

Set fixed width to the second column, 300px;

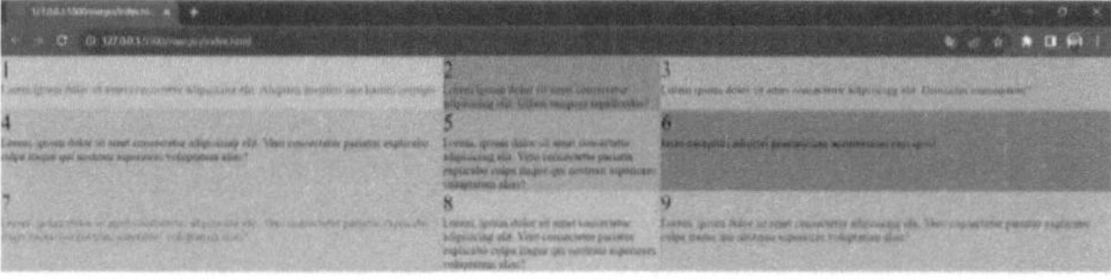

```css
.wrapper {
  display: grid;
  grid-template-columns: auto 300px auto;
}
```

%

Set the third column to be 50% of the container width:

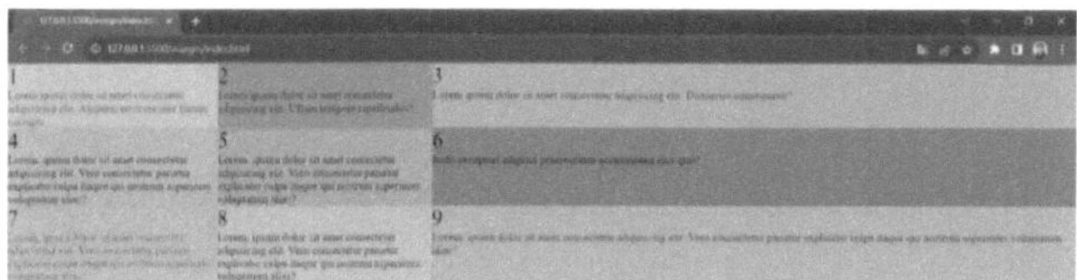

```css
.wrapper {
  display: grid;
  grid-template-columns: auto auto 60%;
}
```

fr

The `fr` unit represents a fraction of the available space
in the grid container.

Set the the third column to be 3 times larger than the second column, while giving the first column fixed 500px:

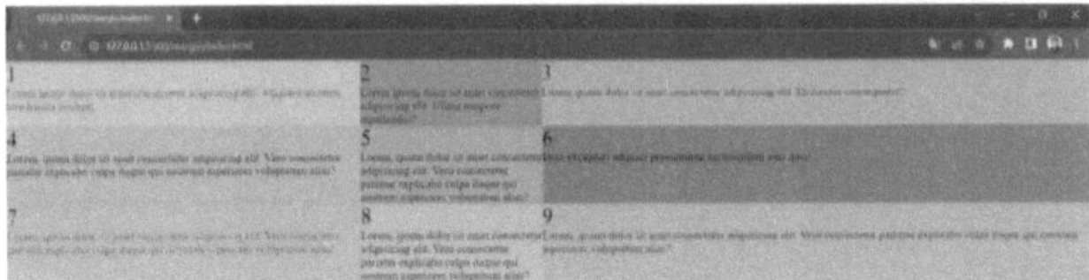

```css
.wrapper {
  display: grid;
  grid-template-columns: 500px 1fr 3fr;
}
```

Grid lines

First you need to know about grid lines.

Grid lines are created when you define tracks in the CSS Grid Layout.

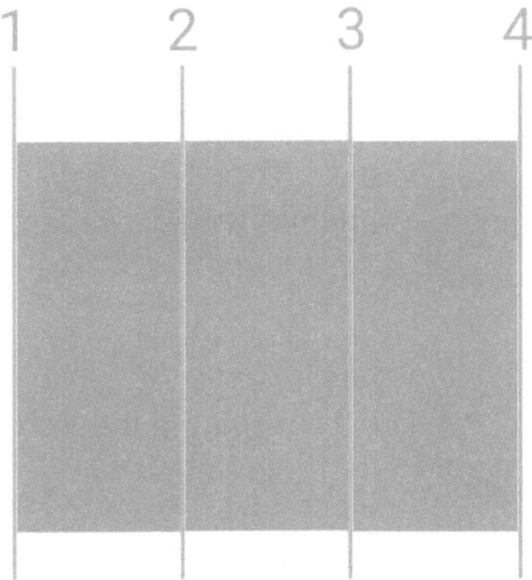

Here are the grid lines for a 3-column layout.

The same applies to the rows.

We use grid lines to determine the start and end for each grid element.

grid-column

The grid-column property defines the size and position of a grid element in a grid layout and is a short form for the grid-column-start and grid-column-end properties.

auto

Default value. The item will be placed following the flow

span n

Specifies the number of columns the item will span

column-line

Specifies in which column the display of the element should begin or end

grid-row

The grid-row property defines the size and position of a grid element in a grid layout and is a short form for the grid-row-start and grid-row-end properties

auto

Default value. The item will be placed following the flow

span n

Specifies the number of rows the item will span

row-line

Specifies in which row the display of the element should begin or end

auto

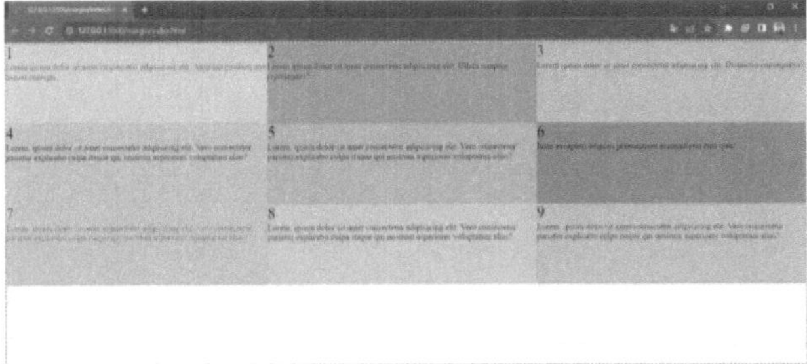

```css
.div-1 {
  background-color: aqua;
  grid-column: auto;
  grid-row: auto;
}
```

span n

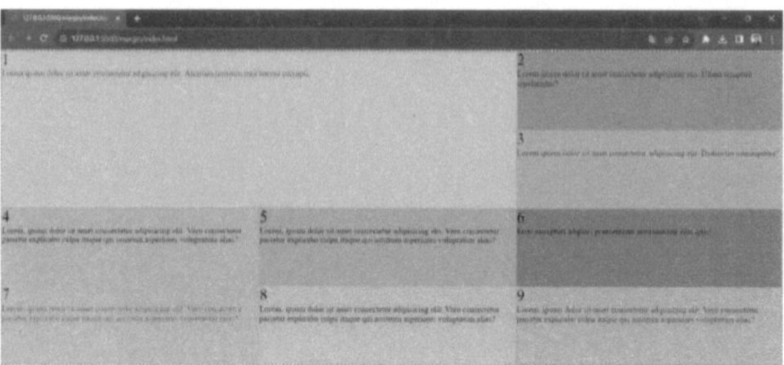

```
.div-1 {
  background-color: aqua;
  grid-column: 1 / span 2;
  grid-row: 1 / span 2;
}
```

justify-content

The CSS property justify-content determines how the
browser distributes the space between and around
content elements along the inline axis of a grid
container.

start or flex-start

Default value. Items are positioned at the beginning of
the container

`flex-start` is specific to flex layout, but if you use it
with grid layout, it will be treated as `start`.

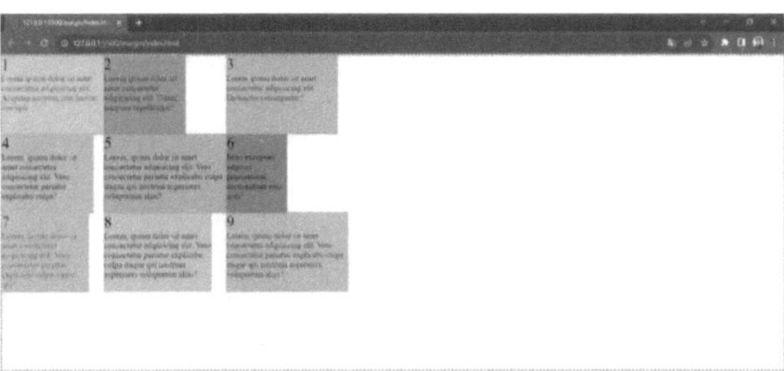

---

end or flex-end

Items are positioned at the end of the container

`flex-end` is specific to flex layout, but if you use it with
grid layout, it will be treated as `end`.

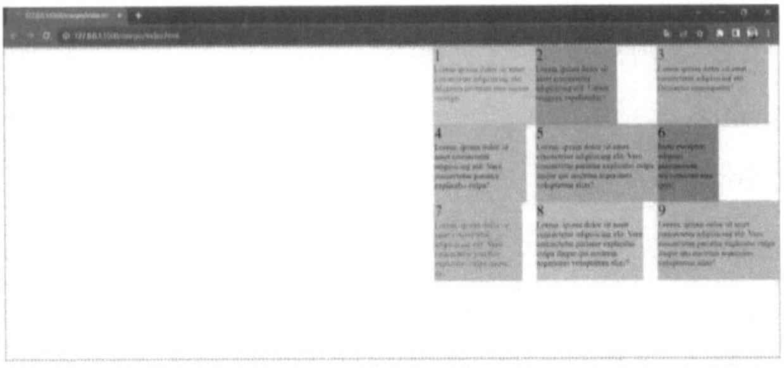

```css
.wrapper {
  display: grid;
  grid-template-columns: auto auto auto;
  grid-template-rows: repeat(4, 150px);
  border: 3px dashed orangered;
  justify-content: end;
}
```

center

Items are positioned in the center of the container

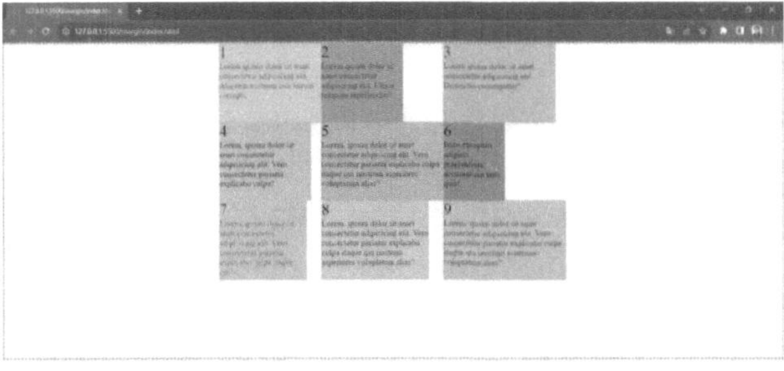

```css
.wrapper {
  display: grid;
  grid-template-columns: auto auto auto;
  grid-template-rows: repeat(4, 150px);
  border: 3px dashed orangered;
  justify-content: center;
}
```

..

Please read my book **"CSS Grid Layout"** to learn all about the grid layout.

Media queries

CSS Media Queries are a feature of CSS that allows you to apply specific styles to a web page based on the characteristics of the user's device or viewport. These characteristics include width, height, alignment, resolution and more.

Media queries are introduced with the keyword @media and can be used for a variety of use cases. They allow you to create responsive designs that adapt to different devices and screen sizes. With the help of media queries, you can design your website differently for users browsing on devices such as smartphones or tablets without changing the actual content of the page.

Media queries consist of a media type (e.g. "Screen", "Print" or "Speech") and one or more expressions, the so-called media features. You can use the media features to influence certain properties of the device or the user's viewport, such as the screen width or orientation. Multiple queries can be combined with logical operators such as "and", "or" and "not".

If a media query is true, the styles specified in the query are applied to the web page. If a media query is false, the styles of this query are not applied. In this way, you can create different layouts, adjust the font size, show or hide elements and much more, depending on the properties of the device or the user's viewport.

Media queries are a fundamental part of responsive web design. They allow you to apply different CSS styles based on the characteristics of the user's device, such as screen size, resolution, or orientation.

Media queries are written using the @media rule and can be used to target specific device features or ranges of values.

```
    /* CSS for screens with a maximum width of
600px */
    @media (max-width: 600px) {
      /* Styles for mobile devices */
    }
```

Here's an example:

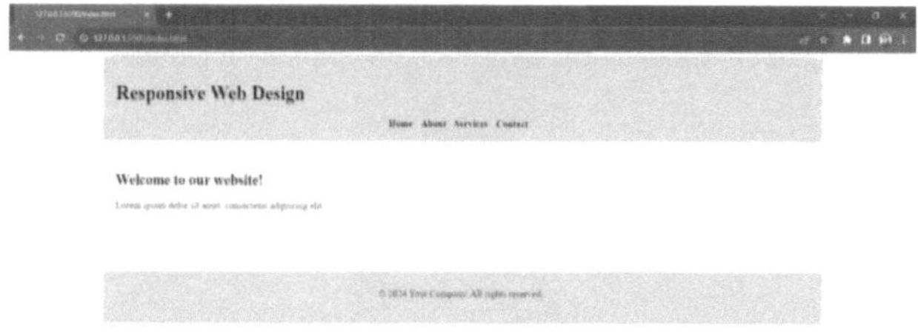

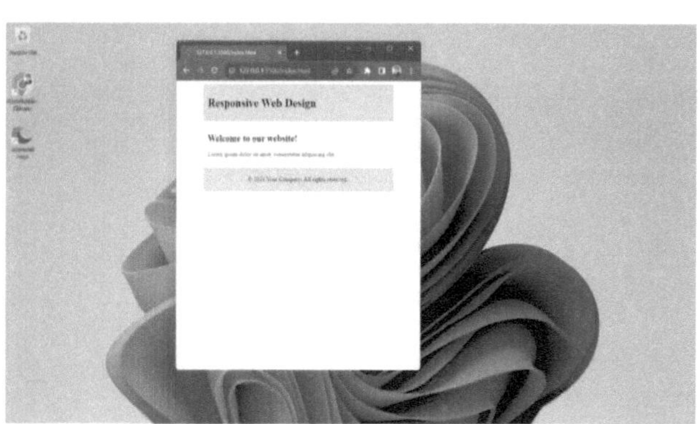

```css
<style>
  .wrapper {
    width: 80%;
    margin: 0 auto;
  }
  header {
    background-color: lightgray;
    padding: 20px;
  }
  h1 {
    font-size: 2em;
  }
  nav ul {
    list-style: none;
    margin: 0;
    padding: 0;
    text-align: center;
  }
  nav li {
    display: inline-block;
    margin-right: 10px;
  }
  nav a {
    text-decoration: none;
    color: black;
    font-weight: bold;
```

```css
}
section {
  padding: 20px;
}
h2 {
  font-size: 1.5em;
}
p {
  font-size: 1em;
}
footer {
  background-color: lightgray;
  padding: 10px;
  text-align: center;
}
@media (max-width: 768px) {
  header {
    padding: 10px;
  }
  h1 {
    font-size: 1.5em;
  }
  nav {
    display: none;
  }
  section {
```

```css
    padding: 10px;
  }
  h2 {
    font-size: 1.2em;
  }
  p {
    font-size: 0.8em;
  }
  footer {
    padding: 5px;
  }
}
@media (min-width: 769px) {
  header {
    height: 100px;
  }
  nav {
    margin-top: 20px;
  }
  h2 {
    margin-top: 30px;
  }
  p {
    margin-bottom: 30px;
  }
  footer {
```

```
      margin-top: 50px;
    }
  }
```
</style>

In this example, the HTML structure includes a container element with a header, navigation, a section, and a footer.

The CSS styles set the width of the container and center it horizontally. Different elements like header, h1, nav, ul, li, a, section, h2, p, and footer are styled accordingly. Media queries are used to apply different styles based on screen size:

- Small screens: (max-width: 768px)
    - Styles for the header, h1, nav, section, h2, p, and footer are adjusted to optimize the layout for smaller screens. For example, the padding and font sizes are reduced to accommodate the limited space, and the navigation is hidden (display: none) to provide a more compact layout.
- Medium screens: (min-width: 769px)
    - Styles for the header, nav, h2, p, and footer are adjusted to provide a more

spacious layout suitable for medium-sized screens. For example, the height of the header is increased, margin and padding values are adjusted, and additional spacing is added around the heading, paragraph, and footer.

Multi-column layout (for newspapers and magazines)

CSS Multi-column layout is a feature that allows you to divide content into multiple columns, similar to what you see in newspapers and magazines. It provides a way to create a more readable and visually appealing layout for long-form content.

CSS3 Multi-column Layout provides an effective way to organize text content into multiple columns, improving readability and user experience. It's particularly useful for presenting articles, blog posts, and other text-heavy content. By applying the appropriate properties, you can customize the column count, gap, rules, and spanning to create visually appealing and well-structured multi-column layouts.

This is applied directly to the element containing the text;

To use the multi-column layout, set the number of columns to a value as follows.

column-count: 5;

column-count

The column-count property specifies the number of columns an element should be divided into.

auto

Default value. The number of columns is determined by other properties, such as column-width

---

```
<style>
  .wrapper {
    font-size: 20px;
```

```css
        column-count: auto;
    }
</style>
```

number

The optimum number of columns into which the content of the element should flow

```css
.wrapper {
    font-size: 20px;
    column-count: 5;
}
```

column-gap

The column-gap CSS property sets the size of the gap (gutter) between an element's columns.

```css
.wrapper {
  font-size: 20px;
  column-count: 5;
  column-gap: 30px;
}
```

column-rule

The column-rule property sets the width, style, and color of the rule between columns.

It is a shorthand for the following CSS properties

<column-rule-width> <column-rule-style (required)> <column-rule-color>

column-rule: <column-rule-width> <column-rule-style (required)> <column-rule-color>

```css
.wrapper {
  font-size: 20px;
  column-count: 5;
  column-gap: 30px;
  column-rule: 3px dotted blue;
}
```

column-span

The CSS property column-span allows an element to span across all columns if its value is set to all.

none

Default value. The element should span across one column

```
<style>
  .wrapper {
    font-size: 20px;
    column-count: 5;
    column-gap: 30px;
    column-rule: 3px dotted blue;
  }
  .header {
    background-color: darkviolet;
    color: white;
    font-size: 24px;
    column-span: none;
  }
</style>
```

all

The element should span across all columns

```css
.header {
  background-color: darkviolet;
  color: white;
  font-size: 24px;
  column-span: all;
}
```

column-fill

The CSS property column-fill controls how the content of an element is balanced when it is split into columns.

balance

Content is equally divided between columns.

```css
.wrapper {
  font-size: 20px;
  column-count: 5;
  column-gap: 30px;
  column-rule: 3px dotted blue;
  column-fill: balance;
}
```

auto

Columns are filled sequentially.

```css
.wrapper {
  font-size: 20px;
  column-count: 5;
  column-gap: 30px;
  column-rule: 3px dotted blue;
  column-fill: auto;
}
```

Let's define a fixed height for the container and check again

balance

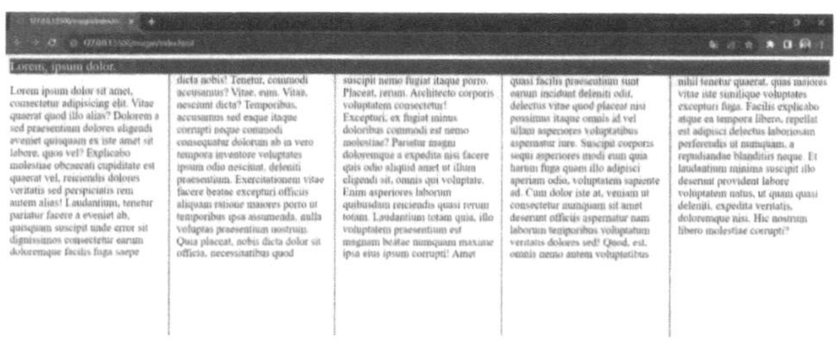

```css
.wrapper {
  font-size: 20px;
  column-count: 5;
  column-gap: 30px;
  column-rule: 3px dotted blue;
  height: 500px;
  column-fill: balance;
}
```

auto

```
.wrapper {
  font-size: 20px;
  column-count: 5;
  column-gap: 30px;
  column-rule: 3px dotted blue;
  height: 500px;
  column-fill: auto;
}
```

Column Breaks

CSS column breaks are properties that allow you to control how content is divided and displayed in multi-column layouts. They specify where columns should break, whether content should be forced to a new column or page, and how to handle column-spanning elements.

break-before

The break-before property determines whether a page break, a column break or a region break should occur before the specified element.

avoid

Avoid a page/column/region break before the element

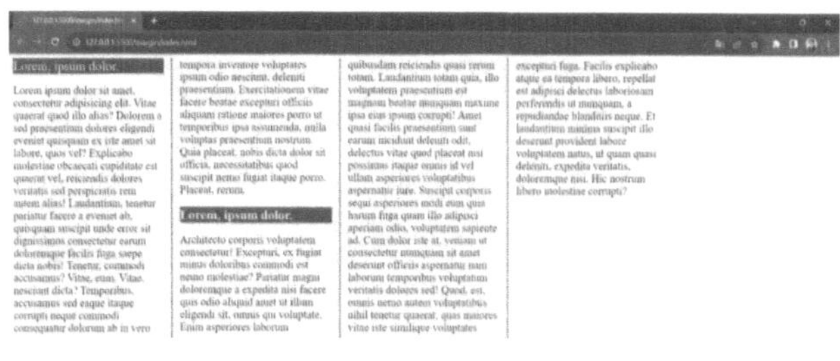

```
<style>
  .wrapper {
    font-size: 20px;
    column-count: 5;
    column-gap: 30px;
    column-rule: 3px dotted blue;
    height: 500px;
```

```css
    column-fill: auto;
  }

  .header {
    background-color: darkviolet;
    color: white;
    font-size: 24px;
    column-span: none;
  }

  .title-break {
    background-color: darkviolet;
    color: white;
    font-size: 24px;
    break-before: avoid;
  }
</style>
```

column

Always insert a column-break before the element

```css
.title-break {
  background-color: darkviolet;
  color: white;
  font-size: 24px;
  break-before: column;
}
```

Responsive images

CSS provides several tools and properties for creating responsive images. These tools allow you to display different versions of an image depending on the device or screen size, ensuring that the image looks good and loads quickly on all devices.

srcset and sizes attributes in HTML
The srcset and sizes attributes are used in HTML to provide multiple image sources and hints to help the browser choose the appropriate image to display based on the device's resolution and viewport size.

The srcset attribute allows you to specify multiple image sources with different resolutions. The browser uses this information to select the most appropriate image to download and display. The sizes attribute is used to define the size of the image element and can be a fixed size or relative to the viewport width.

Here's an example of how to use the srcset and sizes attributes in HTML:

HTML
```html
<img src="image.jpg" srcset="image-2x.jpg 2x,
image-3x.jpg 3x" sizes="(min-width: 600px)
50vw, 100vw" alt="Responsive Image">
```

In this example, the src attribute specifies the default image source. The srcset attribute provides two additional image sources, image-2x.jpg and image-3x.jpg, with descriptors indicating their pixel density. The sizes attribute specifies that the image should be 50% of the viewport width when the viewport is at least 600px wide, and 100% of the viewport width otherwise.

object-fit and object-position properties in CSS
The object-fit and object-position properties in CSS are used to control how an image behaves within its container.

The object-fit property determines how the image is resized or cropped to fit its container. It can take values like fill, contain, cover, none, or scale-down. For example, object-fit: cover will resize the image to cover the entire container while maintaining its aspect ratio.

The object-position property allows you to adjust the position of the image within its container. It can take values like top, bottom, left, right, or a combination of these. For example, object-position: center will center the image within its container.

Here's an example of how to use the object-fit and object-position properties in CSS:

<u>**css**</u>

```css
img {
  width: 100%;
  height: 300px;
  object-fit: cover;
  object-position: center;
}
```

In this example, the image will be resized to cover the entire container while maintaining its aspect ratio (object-fit: cover). The object-position: center property ensures that the image is centered within the container.

Fluid typography (vw, vh, clamp())

Fluid typography refers to the technique of adjusting the font size based on the screen size or viewport dimensions. It allows the font size to scale smoothly and responsively, ensuring optimal readability and user experience across different devices and screen sizes.

There are several CSS properties and functions that can be used to implement fluid typography, including the viewport width (vw) and viewport height (vh) units, as well as the clamp() function.

Viewport Width (vw) and Viewport Height (vh) Units:
- The vw unit represents a percentage of the viewport width, while the vh unit represents a percentage of the viewport height.
- For example, if you set a font size to 2vw, it will be 2% of the viewport width. Similarly, 2vh will be 2% of the viewport height.
- By using vw and vh units, the font size can automatically adjust based on the size of the viewport, providing a fluid and responsive typography experience.

The clamp() Function:
- The clamp() function is a CSS function that allows you to set a range of values for a property, with a preferred value in the middle.
- It takes three parameters: a minimum value, a preferred value, and a maximum value.
- The preferred value is the value that will be used if it falls within the range defined by the minimum and maximum values.
- The clamp() function is particularly useful for implementing fluid typography because it allows you to set a minimum and maximum font size, while the preferred font size adjusts based on the viewport size.
- For example, clamp(16px, 5vw, 24px) sets the font size to be a minimum of 16 pixels, a

preferred size of 5 viewport width units (vw), and a maximum of 24 pixels.

You can also use the relative length units of em, rem and percent.

The calc() function in CSS allows you to perform mathematical calculations within property values. This function is useful for creating dynamic styles that adapt to various factors such as screen size or user interactions.

Media Query Features

CSS media queries are a powerful tool that allow developers to customize the styling of their web content based on various factors, such as screen size, resolution, orientation, and aspect ratio. Let's explore some of the key features of CSS media queries:

min-width and max-width:
- These features are used to target specific ranges of screen resolutions or viewport sizes.
- min-width is used to apply styles when the viewport width is equal to or greater than a specified value.
- max-width is used to apply styles when the viewport width is equal to or less than a specified value.

- By using min-width and max-width together, you can target a specific range of screen resolutions or viewport sizes.

orientation:
- The orientation feature is used to target the orientation of the device, such as portrait or landscape mode.
- It can be used to apply different styles based on the device's orientation.
- For example, you can use @media only screen and (orientation: landscape) to apply styles when the device is in landscape mode.

resolution:
- The resolution feature is used to target the resolution of the device's screen.
- It allows you to apply different styles based on the device's screen resolution.
- You can use min-resolution and max-resolution prefixes to query for minimum and maximum values, respectively.

aspect-ratio:
- The aspect-ratio feature is used to test the aspect ratio of the viewport.
- It represents the width-to-height aspect ratio of the viewport.
- You can use min-aspect-ratio and max-aspect-ratio prefixes to query for minimum and maximum values, respectively.

Conclusion

Congratulations to you! You have read the book "Responsive Design: All CSS functions for adaptive layouts". Now you know all the CSS functions you can use for adaptive layouts. Remember that learning is an ongoing process. Practice makes perfect — build your own projects, experiment with the features you learn, and delve into the extensive online resources.

Thank you for joining me in my exploration of CSS Responsive Design. I wish you the best of luck on your coding journey. Have fun coding and good luck with your applications!

Media Attributions

Postmodern business cover collection
Image by [freepik](#)

Logo template design
Image by [flatart](#) on Freepik

E commerce landing page
Image by [freepik](#)

Mid-century modern living room interior design with monstera tree
Image by [rawpixel.com](#) on Freepik

Gray sofa in living room with copy space
Image by [wuttichai1983](#) on Freepik

Sofa in green living room with copy space
Image by [wuttichai1983](#) on Freepik

A living room with a blue sofa and a gold coffee table.
Image by [chandlervid85](#) on Freepik

Stylish scandinavian living room with design mint sofa furnitures mock up poster map plants and eleg
Image by benzoix on Freepik

Gray sofa in white living room interior with copy space 3D rendering
Image by wuttichai1983 on Freepik

Don't miss out!

Receive an email when Abdelfattah Ragab publishes a new book. It's free and without obligation.

Also by Abdelfattah Ragab

- ◇ CSS Grid Layout
- ◇ CSS Flexbox Layout
- ◇ Angular for Beginners
- ◇ Angular Reactive Forms
- ◇ React Portfolio App Development

About the Author

Abdelfattah Ragab is a professional software developer
with more than 20 years of experience.
https://abdelfattah-ragab.com

About the Publisher

Abdelfattah Ragab is a highly qualified and experienced software developer with over 20 years of experience in the industry. Specializing in front-end development, Abdelfattah Ragab has a deep understanding of Angular, JavaScript, TypeScript, HTML and CSS. Read more at https://abdelfattah-ragab.com

www.ingramcontent.com/pod-product-compliance
Lightning Source LLC
LaVergne TN
LVHW040322200726

843493LV00015B/2448